MY PATH

THROUGH PARALYSIS

Bruce Dunn

*Touchstone Press, 2 Oak St., Suite 4,
Oneonta, NY 13820*

Copyright © 2017, Bruce Dunn

Touchstone Press
PO Box 396, Oneonta, NY 13820
USA

All rights reserved.
No part of this publication may be reproduced,
stored in a retrieval system,
or transmitted in any form or by any means,
electronic, mechanical, photocopying,
recording or otherwise without prior written
permission from Bruce Dunn or his estate.

First Edition November, 2017

ISBN 978-0-9973569-2-2

Printed in the United States of America

Dedication

Rita Daley
A blessing in my life.

Donna Smith
Chief rehab nurse,
She made it seem easy.

Saeed Bajwa, MD
Gifted neurosurgeon
A treasure to his community

Philip Dunn
A very good brother to have.

Special Thanks to:

Barb Dauria and Touchstone Press
This little book would not exist without them.

Dr. Paul Jensen
For his pro bono editing prowess,
(All subsequent errors are my own.)

Extra Special Thanks to:

Mrs. Lillian Smith
For a lifetime of love and support.

There are many others who were
helpful during this difficult journey.
Hopefully, you know who you are.
Mentioned here or not, please believe I
am full of gratitude and sincere appreciation.

> *"Now that I showed you what I been through,*
>
> *Don't take nobody's word what you can do."*
>
> — *John Lennon*

My dog, Sara,

was with me when

my truck rolled...

One...

Two...

Three

times, its roof

crushing down

on us as it went.

Bruce Dunn

CONTENTS

THE CRASH 1

THE INTENSIVE CARE UNIT 15

REHABBING. 37

HOME AGAIN. 71

SARA-INSIGHT. 85
VERTEBRAE DIAGRAM 87
ABOUT THE AUTHOR 91
ACKNOWLEDGEMENTS 94
ORDER THE BOOK. 95

THE CRASH

Saturday, July 9, 1988

It was a warm July morning and I spent it cleaning out under the front porch of the old house. The house was on a west facing hillside in the town of Butternuts, New York. It was situated 1700 feet above sea level, and had a pleasant view of the tree-covered hills across the valley. I bought the house and moved into it the previous November.

I lived there with my dog, Sara, a six year old 80 pound Newfoundland/Golden Retriever cross. I had her since she was a pup, and she made me smile just to look at her. We had been invited to a work/play barbeque that afternoon at Jack's house. I never could have guessed that before that day was done, my life would be forever changed.

My friend and neighbor, Jack, invited Sara and me over for a work/play barbecue. Jack lived in the neighboring town of Laurens. He and I had been friends for a lot of years, and had driven the back roads of south central New York in his pickup truck for many miles. We had a great rapport and drank many beers together. He had recently finished building and moving into his house, but there was a lot of work yet to be done on the property. That was the reason for the gathering. In addition to Jack, Sara and I, Jack's girlfriend, Sue, Sue's mother, and her friend, Bill were there. Later in the afternoon our friend, Mike, came by.

We did a bit of yard work, but mostly ate and drank beer. Toward evening a bonfire was started, and Jack used the back blade of his tractor to push a pile of brush into the fire. I don't recall much beyond that. There is a vague glimpse of a memory of someone going out for more beer; and one of saying goodbye to Jack, Bill and Mike.

I used to temper my beer drinking with a little pot, if I had any, but Mike didn't use it, and I had never met Bill before, so I didn't use it. As a result, or perhaps as an excuse, I drank a lot more than usual that evening.

The party broke up around eleven thirty. I knew I'd had too much to drink and thought it best not to drive home on the busier county road. No sense in putting someone else in harm's way. Instead, I decided to take the seasonal one-lane road through the woods.

Very few people used the seasonal road and I was pretty sure no one else would be driving on it that late at night. Jack lived on Starr Road and to access the woods road from his house I had to bear right where Starr Road curved left. I had taken the seasonal road home numerous times, and it promised to be an easy drive. It was a 3 mile drive rather than the 4 mile county road, and much more to my liking. It wasn't faster, but it was nice driving through the woods.

Sara and I never made it home. Accident reconstruction had me trying to follow Starr Road where it went left, rather than bearing right on to the seasonal road as I'd planned. Because of excess speed I failed to make the turn and went off the road into a field. This explanation has always baffled me, as my intention had been to bear right at the seasonal road and not follow Starr Road as it curved left. Perhaps a deer was in the way and that caused me to change course.

Vehicle Direction of Travel

Between the road and the field was a drainage ditch, and as my vehicle left the road, the outside of the right front tire impacted the far side of the drainage ditch. This collision sent the small truck into a roll.

The Daily Star newspaper report said my truck rolled three times. When the roof of the truck came into contact with the ground its roof supports failed, and the roof collapsed with me and the dog under it. I later found the wrecked vehicle in a junk yard and sat in it. Most of my head stuck out of the now busted out sunroof.

My Path Through Paralysis

My Isuzu Truck, pre-crash

There is much I have been told about the next two weeks for which I have no personal recollection. It is as though four hours before injury and two weeks post injury have been wiped from my memory. I spent many hours and dollars talking to Jack from the hospital trying to figure out how my accident happened.

Only after I returned home did I learn that gravel spread by the town highway crew was especially thick at that corner. This helped me understand how I had lost control. The accident happened in a rural area late at night. It was my great good fortune that a man and a woman were camped out at a small abandoned stone quarry less than a hundred yards from the crash site. They heard the crash and investigated. The man then went to the house at the top of the field and woke the people there. They made the appropriate phone call and help was soon on its way. I later spoke with the owner of the house and apologized for tearing up his yard. He laughed off my apology and asked me how I was. He said my limbs had been spastic that night.

The ambulance and emergency medical team arrived a bit after midnight. My vehicle had come to rest with the driver's door down. Everything was so badly damaged it took over an hour of bending, prying, and cutting to extricate me from the truck.

My consciousness was judged to be coma/stupor for much of this, and my blood pressure had dropped to eighty over sixty. After several attempts, fluids were administered intravenously, and my condition began to stabilize. By the time we got to the Fox Hospital emergency room my blood pressure and consciousness were no longer a major concern, although the time I spent there was recorded on Code Blue Documentation.

I guess bad news travels fast, because by the time the emergency medical team got me on my way quite a few people had gathered at the scene of the crash. Jack was there and he later told me that Sara's only injury was a long wide scratch on her snout.

One of the volunteers or onlookers at the site took Sara home with him that night. Jack said he would see this guy's truck from time to time and Sara would be sitting in the passenger seat. Looking back, I'm okay with the fact that this guy took her. He obviously liked her, but he didn't know Jack or me, and had no way of knowing there wasn't someone home to take care of her. He liked her and took her. She even replaced the dog that used to ride with him in his truck.

A week or two before I came home from the hospital Jack looked this guy up and got my dog back for me. On recollecting, I feel bad for the guy. She was a wonderful dog and he had her for over six months. He had probably gotten quite attached to her. But giving her up never occurred to me. I couldn't have done it anyhow.

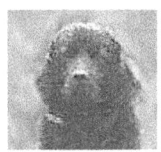

Sara

It was determined by the emergency room doctor that I needed to go to a trauma center. The nearest one was at Wilson Memorial Hospital in Johnson City, New York. A call was made to Wilson Hospital and they made ready to receive me. The emergency squad that had thus far handled me now transported me to Wilson Hospital with a nurse on board. We departed from Fox at 3:45 am and arrived at the trauma center one hour and fifteen minutes later. My blood pressure started to drop again and was treated a second time with intravenous fluids. My condition was described as "awake, confused, disoriented". I was moaning, "I can't breathe" and "Please, can I roll on my side?"

Once I was at Wilson Hospital, I was intubated, that is a tube was placed in my mouth and down my throat to my lungs to help me breathe. Shortly after, my left lung failed and a chest tube was inserted. Doctors' notes recorded that the wounds to my head and neck were extensively cleaned of "pine needles, grass, rocks, stones, and gravel."

The x-rays of my cervical spine showed two badly fractured and dislocated discs, C-6 and C-7. Instead of C-6 being positioned above C-7, it was now located sideways to it. There was no neurological activity below C-6, but there was some at my biceps. I could move my right arm and had a small amount of grip with that hand, but no strength at all with my left hand.

Chest x-rays revealed two broken ribs and contusions on both lungs. There were fractures to the left clavicle and scapula, and cuts and scrapes on my forehead, left ear and the left side of my neck. My right ear was nearly separated from my head. It took ten inches of suture line to close the various cuts, and repair the ear.

A physical exam note at the time described a "well built, healthy looking man lying in severe distress on the Stryker frame." When this accident happened I was in good physical condition. When not at my job at the group home (for developmentally disabled adults) I devoted myself to working on my recently acquired fixer upper home. I had been hard working outside since spring and spent the prior two weeks thinning out a small woodlot behind the house. As a result, I was strong, and more than a few professionals told me that this helped me survive.

The Stryker frame I was lying on is a medical device that has two parts, a top and a bottom. It encloses the body the way bread encloses the filling in a sandwich. There is an opening for the face similar to the type of table that massage therapists and acupuncturists use. The frame is used for turning a body over without any of the body parts being moved. With a couple people at each end of the frame I would be turned over so now I was facing down instead of up, then back again as needed. Being paralyzed and entirely dependent on the competency of others, getting flipped in a Stryker frame was a scary thing for me.

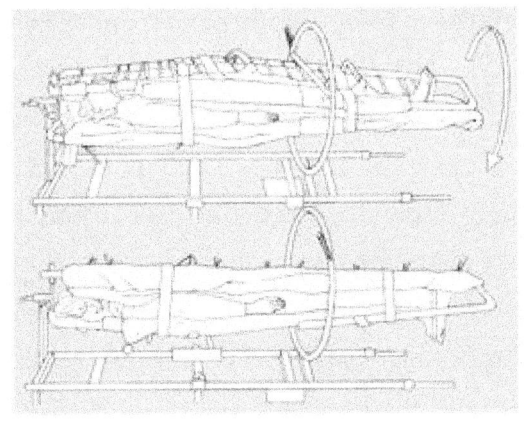

Stryker Frame

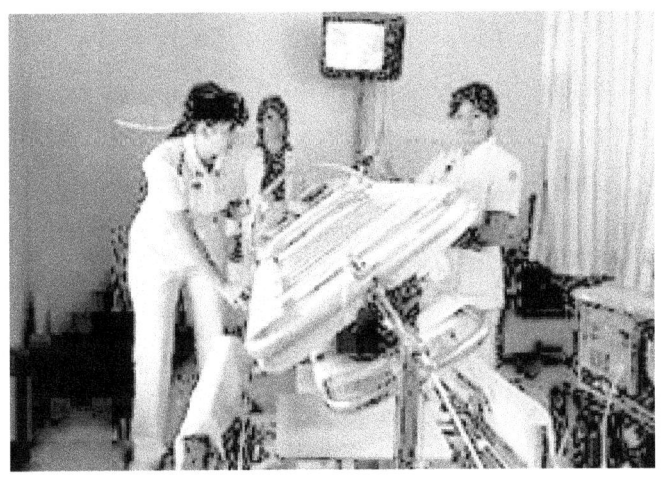

Stryker Frame in use.

To treat my broken neck the neurosurgeon placed tongs on my head from which weight could be hung and traction applied. This device is often referred to as a halo because it is round and fits over top of one's head. The halo itself doesn't actually touch the head, but is positioned slightly above it, and held securely in place by four screws anchored into the skull at approximately equal distance from each other. I don't remember it being installed and I'm glad I don't. It would be many months before the awful thing came off. It was hard to like.

For four weeks I was in the intensive care unit. During the three and a half weeks before my stabilization surgery, I was flat on my back, my head immobile, with twenty nine pounds of weights hanging from a pulley and pulling on my spinal column. Before the weight was applied there was no neurological activity below C-6, because my spinal cord had become pinched.

The traction applied with the weights stretched my neck, realigned the vertebrae and removed pressure on my spinal cord. This allowed neurological impulses to again occur below level C-6 (see diagram page 86). I began to get neurological return.

Neurological activity had been shut down for about seven hours, and real damage had occurred, both in the cord and below it. A spinal cord injury at the cervical level raises absolute hell with a body. It doesn't leave a stone unturned as to the things it affects and the damage it does. When cord cells die, they are not replenished. When they are gone, they are gone for good.

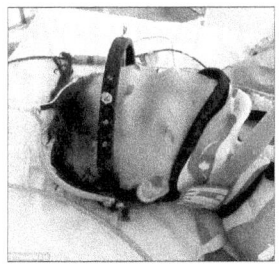

Note this patient has a line attached to top of head with weight to keep spine open, similar to mine.

In traction

THE INTENSIVE CARE UNIT

Much happened in the ICU. In the early days it was all I could do just to be. When I learned that my friend, Rita, had been staying overnight in the hospital, I made her promise me to go home, because I couldn't afford the mental energy it took to worry after her. The medical chart at the end of the bed called for bed rest, and that is exactly what was needed. My body had received an enormous shock and required time to heal.

It was a couple weeks before I came around to a full state of consciousness, or at least the memory of one. Family and friends made for a steady stream of visitors. It is hard to overstate the worth and value these visits had for me. My sister brought my daughter, who was then in her teens, and they stayed at my house. My sister is the one who gave permission in the early morning hours after the crash to allow for medical procedures to begin.

Sister Nancy

Neither was surprised by what had happened, and I'm pretty sure my daughter was angry with me.

Two of my brothers were coordinating their visits to me to be sure I had company at least every other day. It was a four hundred mile round trip for them. Also friends from home came regularly although it was a hundred thirty, hundred forty mile round trip for them. It was all helpful, humbling, and healing. I was described in these early days by two of my visitors as looking like I had been "pulled through a knothole" and "like a baby bird that had fallen from its nest."

Jack did all that could be expected from a friend. He visited often, but more than that, he also took care of my house for the nearly seven months I was gone. He mowed the grass, collected the mail, paid my bills, and kept heat in the house when it got cold. He had his eye on things and kept the place looking like it was lived-in, the better to avoid unwanted attention from less than honorable people. In the early days he was consumed with guilt about letting me drive home knowing I was drunk.

One of my earliest memories is of the nurses telling me to stop touching my bandaged right ear. I was told several times, and each time assured them with absolute sincerity that I had not touched it, even as my fingers, stained red from the Betadine gave me away. As a result, my right arm was secured to the bedside. My left arm wasn't working, so it wasn't a problem.

I was a bit of an irritant to the nurses because I kept asking them what happened to me. They would tell me and a few minutes later I would ask again. I was confused for a long time and had problems discerning reality even longer. For instance, I was sure the hospital was built on sacred ground, that witchcraft caused me to crash, and my injuries were due to God having given me a good swat.

Very early on I would break out crying for no apparent reason. I think now it was because I was going through all the reasons why my current situation of being paralyzed and in an intensive care unit couldn't be possible, only to come to the inescapable conclusion that it was true. The realization made me cry.

Rita didn't drive then and often came with Jack to see me, but sometimes she came on the bus. She loved me more than I knew, but at that time had depression and I was afraid of becoming involved with someone who had emotional difficulties. Once, her work friend, Marion, brought Rita to visit me. I knew Marion as I had also worked with her. She was very down to earth, and we liked each other in a joking kind of way. When Marion saw me lying there, she looked at me as if to say, "What happened to you?" I couldn't speak because of being intubated, and so used a letter board to communicate. I spelled my answer out one letter at a time. "I FUCKED UP".

I never kidded myself about what I had done, at least when I was in my right mind. It was an incredibly stupid thing that couldn't be undone. I had destroyed my vehicle and nearly my life. I was an embarrassment to my daughter and a burden to friends and family. Worst of all, I felt a complete loss of face and trying to recover some of that became a motivation for me. I had to pull myself out of the hole I was in, so I could participate in life again. From the very beginning of my hospitalization I knew with certainty I would regain the ability to walk. I also knew it would take everything I could possibly do to make it happen. I became a man on a mission and told everyone who would listen that I would recover from the paralysis and walk again.

One nurse disagreed with me and said I was too much of a wimp to succeed with rehabilitation. She felt that way because at the time I couldn't cough as hard as I'd been instructed to. Then I had a lot of mucous in my lungs, especially the left one where the broken ribs were. Staff was always telling me to breathe deep and cough hard. I wanted the stuff out of my lungs in the worst way, but every time I breathed deep and coughed hard, I felt as though I was being stabbed with an ice pick. I couldn't do it.

But I knew something that nurse didn't know. I was not a wimp, and I didn't lack courage, either. The young man in x-ray whom I'd become friendly with assessed me just right. He said, "You're the one who is going to show the doctors up, because you want to get better." I wanted to get better more than anything.

From the very beginning I had two therapists, one physical and one occupational. The physical therapist would come around in the morning and move my limbs through their range of motion. She instructed me to exercise the body parts that worked, and to try to move those parts that didn't work. I did as I was told and added exercises of my own, moving each body part one hundred times. One afternoon while doing my exercises I tried to move the big toe on my right foot, and I thought I felt it move. I called the nurse in to verify and she said, "Yes, only just perceptible, but it moved." This was momentous. It meant there was neurological return to my right leg. The cord damage was asymmetrical, injuring my right leg more than my left and my left arm more than my right. This was inconvenient as I am left handed and right footed, but it didn't seem to matter at the time.

A few days before the operation to stabilize my neck the surgeon told me that in addition to the nerve damage from the spinal cord there was "isolated" nerve damage at the site of the fracture. The nerves serving the left side of my neck and my left shoulder were injured. In helping me to understand the implications of this, the physical therapist said my arm and shoulder would never be very functional. She said I should become right handed and purchase a typewriter. She told Rita that my disability was so serious that she should find herself another boyfriend. Her comment pissed me off not a little, and she became an enduring source of inspiration as I moved through rehabilitation. I was determined that one day I would return to Wilson Hospital to visit this therapist, and I would take my left arm and hand, and I would punch her with it. I became right handed for a time, until it occurred to me that if my left side is the weakest, it should be used more often, not less. So, I went back to being left handed.

My experience with the occupational therapist was also not good. She wanted to hook me up with all sorts of devices designed to help me function better. I was having none of it. I wanted first to work with what I had, and if it turned out I needed some helpful devices, only then would I consider it. I never did need any of them, except for the typewriter.

My right arm and hand continued to be mischievous when it wasn't restrained. When the plastic surgeon came to remove the stitches from my right ear, the tube that had been in my nose was lying across my chest. I have this vague memory of holding it out in front of me, this bloody, mucous covered tube and feeling rather proud of myself that I had removed it. It was due to come out that day anyhow, so no harm was done.

Once all the tubes were out, I could talk again, and take solid food. One of the foods that Rita found and brought for me was a well toasted, buttered bagel. I was really looking forward to eating it, but the big doses of antibiotics I was taking caused the inside of my mouth to be full of thrush, (hundreds and hundreds of tiny blisters throughout my mouth) that couldn't tolerate the hard edges of the bagel. It went uneaten.

Thrush from the antibiotics was not the only drug side effect that caused me problems. I was being dosed regularly with morphine, for pain and sedation. Morphine is constipating. It had been close to three weeks since my last bowel movement. Besides being painful, in my deluded state, I believed if I couldn't move my bowel it would kill me. Nursing staff knew of my problem and every day offered a new solution, but nothing worked. I was scared to death.

I talked Rita into bringing me two boxes of Ex Lax. I read the instructions and took a full box of the chocolate with a cup of coffee. Then I took half of the second box. It was a hurtful, unpleasant experience, but when it was over I no longer felt like I was going to die.

There were a couple bright spots in intensive care. One of them was Martha, the cleaning lady. She always had time for a word. One of my favorite music albums from back in the day was the Beatles' white album, and one of my favorite songs therein was "Martha." It's a very pretty song.

I asked Martha if she was familiar with it, and she was not. I decided to get her the white album so she could hear her song. I had my intrepid friend and girl Friday, Rita, go on a mission to find the white album as a gift for Martha. Rita was good like that.

All I knew of my surroundings was the ceiling above me and the bed under. I knew nothing about what existed beyond that. Asking Rita to find a copy of the Beatle's white album was no small request, and yet she found it. She always found what I thought I needed. And Martha got to hear a song I'd chosen just for her.

Another bright spot was the company of a most beautiful young doctor-in-training. She visited four or five times towards the end of my stay and would stay for about an hour. Her eyes were so easy to fall into that I found myself telling her my life story, about how I got to be, not just in hospital, but in upstate New York. As I talked, I listened and learned. I didn't just reveal myself to her, I revealed myself to me. I had never really come home from the war. I didn't feel like I belonged anymore. I was unsettled, and drank too much. I supported myself and was usually married, even if with different spouses; but I was more out of control than not.

Lying there in the hospital felt like coming home. I looked back over my life and found myself wanting. I wished I had tried harder at life, had done my best, especially in school; but I had not. Past would not be prelude. When it came time for the beautiful young doctor and I to part, she said she learned a lot from me. I wish I knew what it was.

The month of July, 1988, was very hot, and the intensive care unit was no exception. As the weeks went by and my condition improved I was able to move my body around on the bed a little. On one occasion I was able to get my back side out from under the sheet, and it was some relief from the heat. I knew my bare behind was sticking out, and while I am usually a modest guy, this time it didn't matter. When the nurse noticed, she covered me up. I had lost about a third of my body weight, but she said, "Good thing it's a nice one," which made me smile. It still makes me smile, thinking how kind she was. If she had never seen a bony butt before, she certainly saw one that day.

When the neurosurgeon told me what he thought had happened to my neck, I nearly became physically ill. He said my head had twisted to the point it was almost facing backward. All I could envision was Linda Blair in "The Exorcist" and her head swiveling completely around.

The surgeon explained the pending surgery, and said there was a one in ten chance that something could go seriously awry, possibly resulting in complete paralysis or death. I thought the odds were terrible.

I decided if the outcome was paralysis, I would deal with it at that time, but I needed to prepare my soul in case the outcome was death. What I feared most was becoming a bad earthbound spirit, a bad ghost.

In my right mind I understood I had rolled my vehicle and was injured because of that. When in my delusional state, I believed my most recent former wife had caused me to crash with her mental powers. I knew it was far-fetched even as I thought it, but I thought and believed it nonetheless. In preparation for my possible death, I found it imperative that I harbor no ill will toward my former wife and whatever role she may have had in my crashing.

The Lord's Prayer became a mantra as I prepared myself for surgery. I concentrated on the part about forgiving those who trespass against us. I also used meditation to try to be in my psychic center, to occupy that space, because that's where I wanted to be when my neck was opened up. I practiced breathing slowly and deeply. I had a week or so to get ready and nothing else to do. I was serious, and felt my life depended on it. I wanted to present my surgeon with a body that was utterly calm and relaxed, so he could do his best work.

In anticipation of my possible coming death, I had Rita cut off my beard and shave me. I was certain the Lord didn't want to see me unshaven. When one of the nursing staff saw me clean shaven she was exuberant. She told me how much she disliked men's beards and expressed how "dirty" she thought they were. The way she said "dirty" really creeped me out, and in my defenseless state she made me afraid. She would come into my life again, but not in a bad way.

Since very early on after my injury there had been three basic functions I most wanted back. When life got down to the bare nitty gritty, these are the things that mattered most to me: The first was urination, I wanted to be able to start it and stop it, to have control over it. Second was to have bowels that worked. I didn't want someone else to have to help me with this very basic bodily function. The third was sex. Not least of all, I wanted to experience orgasm again. It all sounds so simple when it's working, but with a spinal cord injury all bets are off.

The day before surgery I thought I could feel urine moving out of me by way of the catheter tube. When the nurse came around I told her. She expressed doubt that I could feel anything, but while we were talking I could feel it again. She pulled back the cover, and sure enough there was amber liquid moving through the tubing. This was an enormously significant event: neurological return, and the beginning of getting my basics back. The day after the operation the catheter was removed, and I've been independent with my bladder function ever since.

I felt good the morning of the operation. Rita was there for support, and I was glad of it. The medication used to prepare me for the operation made slow, deep breathing and centering myself easier, and I was doing fine until I saw my reflection in some overhead chrome. I recognized myself on the gurney, prepped for surgery and being wheeled into the operating room. The reality of what was about to happen hit home, and fear swept over me. The doctor who was responsible for putting me under and keeping me alive during this ordeal was an Asian man; for whom English was not a first language. He used his words sparingly. "Mr. Dunn, very serious operation." He then explained why it was imperative I not cough while he intubated (put that tube down my throat again) me. I stuttered the start of a cough, but it wasn't enough to do any harm. Then, "Mr. Dunn, why you not breathing?", "I'm deep breathing", "Deep breathing fine." It felt like the most intimate exchange I've ever had.

The stabilization surgery involved my lying face down on the Stryker frame. A seven-inch incision was made from the middle of my neck to my upper back. Bone taken from my iliac crest and from the bone bank was placed on each side of my now exposed fractured spinal column. Then the bones were intricately wrapped with wire to hold them in place. The wiring was anchored to disc T-1 on the bottom and disc C-4 on top. Initial plan was to anchor on C-5, but that disk was found to be spider webbed and unstable. (See illustration page 86)

Twice when I was a child, at ages six and seven, I was given ether as an anesthetic, and both times I dreamed of non-stop falling. During this nearly six-hour surgery I dreamed I was an organic gardener on a space station, schooling the doctors on the finer points of gardening. The operation had taken longer than expected, because the damage was greater than anticipated.

As soon as I came out of the anesthesia I tried moving all the body parts that had worked before going into surgery. To my great satisfaction, everything that worked going in worked coming out. I had lost no ground. I immediately exercised everything one hundred times.

I still think often of my surgeon. I'm glad he had been a serious student and became skilled at what he does, instead of living life as if it were but an amusement. Fracture and dislocation is the worst kind of spinal cord injury, but it is the kind from which there is the greatest chance of recovery. I couldn't wait for rehabilitation to begin.

By far the most interesting and unusual thing to happen to me while in intensive care occurred two days after my operation. Although everything had gone well, I was still in bed, in traction with my head immobilized. Unless visitors placed themselves in my direct view, all I could see was the white ceiling above me.

This particular morning a group of nurses or nursing students came around, and the one in charge started cleaning me up while chattering away at the other girls. There was nothing unusual about this; it was part of the morning routine. However, when it came to my genital area, she washed me until I was fully erect. I realized she didn't think I could feel what she was doing.

I knew what she was doing alright, and it was not standard hospital procedure. She was using me to show off for her little entourage. There was a voice that came from the now quiet bedside. It said in a firm defensive tone, "It's not me being bad." It was that young woman who didn't like men's beards.

When I was taken out of traction I was put into a hardened vest that had been custom made for me. The vest had two rods in the front and two in the back that attached to the halo on my head. The rods protruded above my head about two inches and were as big around as a couple of pencils. Its purpose was to keep my neck stable and immobile while the bone grafts healed. It worked well. I could not move my head. This was the second part of the halo. The vest and the poles shooting up through the halo was the brace. Halo and brace. This device looked very technical and "space-agey." It drew comments like, "Do you get good reception with that?" One time in an elevator a priest asked me if I took it off at night. Could he not see it was screwed into my head?

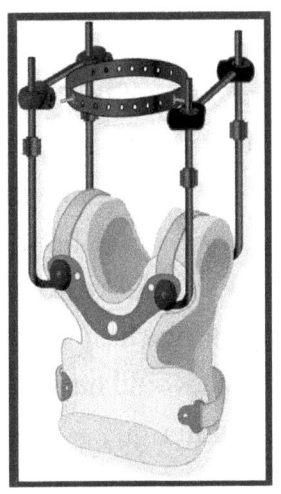

Halo and Brace with Vest

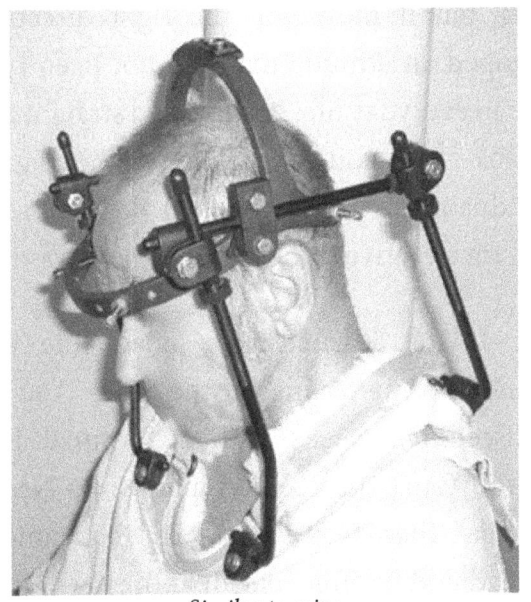

Similar to mine

I transferred out of the intensive care unit to a regular bed for my last couple days at Wilson Memorial. I started feeding myself and with the help of the therapist stood between the parallel bars with my knees locked under me. A primal sound escaped my chest the first time I was helped to stand up. I would hear that sound again in rehab when another guy was helped to stand for the first time.

Progress was achieved in very small increments, but it moved in the right direction. I developed an attitude that had not been typical of me in everyday life: Positive and straight ahead forward. I was going for it and not looking back. If I didn't make it, I'd know I tried. There was no room for negative thinking, and there was none.

I later learned of a book title which summed up my feelings at the time, "You Have Just Been Diagnosed with a Terminal Illness and You Can't Afford the Luxury of a Negative Thought." There was even a song that came into my head and became like an anthem as I moved through recovery. It was an Elton John song, and given the circumstances, a peculiar one, "I'm still standing, yeah, yeah, yeah." Even though I wasn't.

REHABBING

Toward the end of my stay at Wilson Hospital I was twice visited by a physiatrist. A physiatrist is a medical doctor who has specialized in physical rehabilitation. He came to see me to offer the services of the local rehabilitation unit. I had learned there were six spinal cord injury rehabilitation centers in the United States, and one of them was at Thomas Jefferson University Hospital in Philadelphia. I had spent the first twenty one years of my life in south Jersey, about twenty minutes from Jefferson Hospital, and most of my family still lived there. The support of family was important to me, and except for having to pay my own way to get there, rehabbing in Philly seemed the best choice. Besides, there was still a lot about spinal cord injuries that wasn't known. Only four decades earlier people were still dying from broken necks.

The social worker made the arrangements for an ambulance and for transportation to and from the respective airports. For the half minute it took to wheel me from the ambulance to the airplane I felt the air and the sun on my face, and it was the best feeling I'd had in more than a month.

The airplane ride was uneventful, and while I would like to have spent the time looking out the window at the endless mountains of Pennsylvania, I was strapped down to a gurney, and had to settle for a bit of small talk with the nurse who accompanied me.

It had been a month and a day since my injury when I was being checked into the third floor rehabilitation unit at Jefferson Hospital. During the admissions routine physical examination it was discovered I had herpes zoster, also known as shingles, the result of stress and from having had chicken pox as a child.

Shingles is contagious, so instead of being admitted into a regular room with other patients, I was put in a single room and strict isolation procedures were followed. No one came in my room without gown, gloves, and mask. I wasn't allowed to go to the gym. It was a big setback and disappointment. I would be in isolation for nearly two weeks.

One of the nurses who cared for me during my entire stay at Jefferson was a pretty, young woman named Diane. She seemed unaware of how attractive she was, and this naiveté made her all the more charming. I was forty one years old with an absent libido, yet was not unappreciative of a pretty girl.

On one of my first days in isolation, I was brought back to my room in a wheelchair, having been taken somewhere for an appointment. Diane transferred me from the chair to the bed. Because I was dependent on others for almost everything, if there was a way to help, I did so. She was on the small side, but I was so light (my younger brother described my upper arms as being no bigger around than my wrists) she lifted me so my butt was on the edge of the bed, and I helped her by locking my knees under me. By my helping her she misunderstood how much muscle control I had. I had no abdominal muscles working, nothing in the buttocks, and no back muscles. Everything was one hundred per cent out of order. When she let go of me, I fell over like a bowling pin. Fortunately, I fell toward the head of the bed, and no harm was done. Her reaction was "Oops!" But it surely scared me.

Spinal cord injuries are often fraught with complications and mine was no exception. In addition to shingles, I had a pressure sore on my left shoulder blade. The left scapula and clavicle had both been fractured and the clavicle was permanently dislocated. My bony scapula, or shoulder blade, pressed tightly against the skin, and resulted in a sore.

Once the sore was discovered I was instructed to sleep on my right side. For the prior thirty days I laid flat on my back, day and night; now I was to lie only on my right side until the sore healed. As my shingles started to resolve, it was discovered there was a blood clot in my lower right calf, a deep vein thrombosis, or DVT. It was treated with blood thinners, first IV heparin, then Coumadin by mouth. The DVT didn't keep me from the gym when my isolation was over, but it limited what I could do there, because I had to keep the leg elevated.

The bad news just kept on coming, and it was starting to get me down. Additionally, I was continually mildly nauseated from post nasal drip, had anemia, suffered decreased vision in one eye, and had developed temporal mandibular jaw dysfunction which gave me a wicked headache for two days before it was treated. I had a nerve damaged bowel and bladder, bad balance, pharyngitis, a possible closed head injury, and I was wheezing. Could life get any better?

Worst of all were my hands. There is probably nothing that we take more for granted than our opposable thumbs. The experience of having mine not work gave me renewed appreciation for primates. My eating utensils had been built up with foam so I could hold them. My right hand, the good one, was only strong enough to hold a half full can of soda. Much later in out patient physical therapy, I described this problem with my grip to another patient. She told me her grip was so weak she couldn't hold a pencil. Just when you think you have it bad, there is always someone who has it worse. In the gym there was a hand cycle. It had a seat with a sprocket and pedals about chest high. The sprocket was turned with hands on the pedals. My left hand had no grip and was attached to the pedal with Velcro. I'd grip the other pedal with my right hand. I turned it until the sweat ran off me and gradually increased my endurance.

During my hospital experience of just over a hundred fifty days, there were only two people who cared not a whit about my dignity as a fellow human being. One was a woman who put me in mind of a character from "Gone With the Wind", the one that "don't know nothin' 'bout birthin' no babies." She was that useless. I was being toiletted on a commode at the foot of the bed when she stepped out for twenty minutes leaving the door to my room wide open. Every one who walked by could see me sitting there. Thoughts of her still rankle me. The other person was an aid who, when he transported me in a wheelchair, wouldn't close my gown in the back, so my bare back-side showed. I would have liked to kick his lazy inconsiderate ass clear back to where he came from. These were only two out of a hundred or more people, who either cared for me or handled me. Everyone else was good, kind, and competent.

Another of my caretakers was Donna, the nurse in charge of the unit I was assigned to. She was personable and efficient. I came to like her very much and had great respect for her. It had been five weeks since I'd last had a shower and she put me in one. She washed my hair and let the water play on my pressure sore. That first shower was the beginning of the end for the pressure sore, and subsequent showers cleared it up entirely. The shower was definitely the high point of being in isolation. The warm/hot water felt so good that each time I asked the nurses to leave me under until I wrinkled.

Once I was no longer contagious I was put in a regular room with three other patients. Third floor rehab is where people who had a serious spinal cord injury were sent, once they were no longer at death's door. There was no one there just a little bit hurt.

There was a young Asian woman, a senior in college, who had stepped off a trolley into the path of another vehicle. Her injury was at level

C-4, and she had a brush with death while I was there. Today she is an independent, productive member of society. Another young person was pushed down an elevator shaft by his drunken friends. Some patients were victims of circumstance, most were victims of reckless behavior. The stories went on and on. Often alcohol or drugs were involved. I had never before seen such broken people.

My first roommate was a bearded guy a little younger than myself. He had been teaching a friend to drive when the vehicle went over an embankment. His was a complete cervical injury, meaning there was no function below the level of his damaged cord. My injury was incomplete. When I complained my feet were cold, he said he couldn't feel his feet. His father visited often and had grown his beard out in solidarity with his son. On more than one occasion the father said, "I have one more thing to do in life", meaning taking care of his son. From this man I learned what commitment is. I had multiple marriages and never really knew what commitment was. Now I knew.

Thus far, physical and occupational therapy consisted of trying to get me to a place where I could be independent at the activities of daily living. I had a long way to go. I learned how to roll over, to move from lying down to sitting up, from sitting up to transferring to the wheelchair, and from the wheelchair back to bed. I learned how to stand for longer and longer periods, and learned to feed and dress myself.

Dressing myself was more than a little difficult. Putting a sock on my right foot was the hardest. I would do it in two stages. At first I would pull the sock on up to the heel. The effort that it took would so exhaust me I would fall back on the bed to regather my strength. Then I would sit back up and finish pulling it on. The nurse could put on my socks and shoes, then lace and tie my shoes, faster than I could put on one sock. I didn't always refuse help, but mostly I did. As a result, I was often late for morning therapy.

I became independent with the wheelchair and it was a bit of a freedom machine. I used both hands and one foot to propel myself and quickly got pretty good at it.

One day while wheeling around I met Arthur. He took me under his wing and showed me the ropes. Art was tall and very thin. His head was shaved with several big, raw scars on it. His problem was a brain infection, and he never made it out of the hospital, but while he was alive we had some fun. He showed me around the hospital, taught me how to use the elevator, took me down to the hospital lobby where in spite of our rough, frightful appearance, we acted like we belonged. We hung out in the lobby until the door to the street opened, then we wheeled on out of the hospital. We parked ourselves out there and watched the crowd go by. One person tried to force money on us, but we declined. I'm sure our hanging out in front of the hospital broke a lot of rules, but we had some fun with it, and nobody got hurt.

Eventually we went back into the hospital, and Art took me up to the thirteenth floor where there was an enclosed outdoor terrace. It was about ten by thirty feet and had a few tables and chairs. There was a bit of a view and there was hardly anyone ever there. It became my refuge.

Once, when my brothers were visiting me there, another patient came wheeling out and positioned himself at the far end of where we were. In short order we smelled cannabis burning, and this guy was smoking it. My brother, Phil, walked over, introduced himself and asked this guy what was up with him smoking pot. The guy's name was Rob, and he had been injured years before. He had been high up on a ladder when he was electrocuted. He fell to the ground breaking his back and injuring his cord. He experienced violent spasms in his legs, and cannabis worked better than anything else at quieting them down. He said the nurses let him take it in his room if the weather was inclement. It was a case of marijuana being used as medicine in 1988, in Philadelphia, PA.

Another early roommate was Richard. He was a very handsome guy who loved excitement, risk, and racing four wheelers. His injury was at T-1, just below the bottom of the neck, and close to complete. He could no longer feel anything from his chest down. He appreciated how badly he was hurt and said a couple times, "I loved a lot of beautiful girls."

Richard had been hurt when he crashed his motorcycle with his girlfriend on the back. She escaped serious injury, and he was so happy that she wasn't badly hurt. He never complained about his fate with paralysis. He was just glad it hadn't happened to her. It was the same as I felt with my paralysis and injuries. I was only too glad I hadn't done this to somebody else. It would have been so very hard to live with. It used to be my only redeeming thought.

I worked hard at rehabilitation, and the results were beginning to show. Patients who could do more than I when I first got there now couldn't do as much as I.

One roommate, a lawyer, was probably least hurt of anyone there. He was riding his mountain bike in the city and tried to ride up a curb when the front wheel came off, and he fell to the pavement. He refused surgery and did nothing to help himself. If the nurse could do it for him, that's the way he wanted it. He was a demanding, inconsiderate guy who played the television loud into the early hours. He was my worst roommate out of many. His lawyer wife came often to see him. She liked me and respected my effort.

Before becoming a lawyer, she had been a rehab nurse on Jefferson's third floor.

Some people see serious disability as a way of being taken care of for the rest of their lives. It's an allure some can't resist. I think my roommate, however, had his hopes set on a big payday as a paralyzed person in a product liability lawsuit. He left the hospital in a wheelchair, but if he had worked on his rehabilitation, he could have walked off the unit.

Physical and occupational therapy occurred mornings and afternoons for about forty-five minutes per session. For the most part there was no therapy on weekends or holidays, but if something was offered I took it. I was also reading and learning all I could about spinal cord injury.

My brother, Don, had found and purchased for me an excellent book about quadriplegia and paraplegia. It was full of useful information including statistics on who gets injured and when. Typical was a drunk, white guy in his thirties crashing his vehicle on a Saturday night. I was in my forties, but otherwise the shoe fit.

My Brother Don

I learned that the sooner you start to get neurological return, the more you eventually get back. I felt I was in a race for my ability, and had to get recovered as quickly as possible. Questions to my doctors and nurses were endless.

Question authority? Absolutely. I needed to know everything. Nursing and doctor's notes that referenced me during this period often read, "pleasant, cooperative, motivated."

In the late seventies I had developed a diet that would keep me healthy and be a wise use of food dollars. I wouldn't buy any processed food if sugar, salt, or fat was in the first three ingredients. This approach eliminated a lot. In rehab, however, if it had calories I wanted it. I'd lost an incredible amount of weight and needed to gain it back. My healing depended on it.

Rehab food was pretty good. Lemon meringue pie was a mainstay, lunch and dinner, every day. My regular hospital diet was high protein, high calorie, high fiber, and whatever my visitors brought me. My most memorable eating was two ears of buttered and salted corn on the cob wrapped in aluminum foil and still hot, compliments of my niece, Judy, and her husband, Fred. I was gradually gaining weight and getting stronger. I practiced my walking with the aid of the parallel bars.

A couple of weeks after arriving at Jefferson, the unit social worker arranged a family conference in which my diagnosis and functional prognosis would be discussed. In attendance were the social worker, several physiatrists, the therapists, my three brothers, and myself. I was arrogant in those days, and while I hope to not be that way now, then it served me well.

Philip, Me, Don, and Dave

As the conference started I said to the chief physiatrist, "No matter what you tell me, I will do better." He made a comment along the lines of me showing up the doctors. I just nodded and said, "Yeah." He acknowledged I would walk, but said I would need a brace on my right leg. To be fair, my right leg still doesn't work as well as the left. When getting in the car or bathtub, I need to give that leg a hand, but I never wore a brace and I'm very happy to have proven him wrong.

He said I would need four more months of hospitalization, two more with third floor rehab, and two with Jefferson's sister organization, the McGee Institute. The McGee Institute was a free standing rehabilitation hospital that worked with spinal cord injured people to maximize their abilities, and to teach them how to use their wheelchairs most effectively. The thought of four more months in hospital was depressing, but it didn't turn out that way.

My automobile insurance company refused payment of any kind, because alcohol was involved with the crash. My Blue Cross/Blue Shield didn't cover free standing hospitals and McGee wouldn't accept me. It was a big disappointment. As long as I had insurance I needed four more months of therapy, but without insurance I was discharged to my brother Philip's house in six weeks. I could barely ambulate and didn't want to go to my brother's house. He and his wife and daughter had a life that didn't include nursing me, but that's where I went.

Philip became my caretaker and did a good job at it. Every morning he cleaned my rear pin sites. Under my hard plastic vest I wore sheepskin. In order for it to be cleaned I had to lie flat on my back while the vest was opened and the sheepskin removed. After being cleaned it would be put back in place and the vest cinched up tight again. Only then could I move again and get up.

He closed my buttons and helped with so many things, including helping me clean up after an accident I had with my still irregular, unpredictable bowel. Short of doing for him what he did for me, it is a debt that cannot be repaid.

Before being discharged to Philip, I had been out on pass several times and never had any problem with the jostling of the car causing pain at my pin sites. However, when he was driving me to his house after being discharged, every little bump in the road caused excruciating pain there. The fact that this had not happened before caused me great anxiety. After the ride was over, Philip took me to his primary care doctor, and I explained to him what happened and asked him to prescribe something for me should it happen again. I thought being in a halo with a broken neck might engender a little trust or empathy. I was wrong.

He did write a prescription for me, but not before accusing me of coming to him for a legal high. I was irritated by his accusation. I have too much respect for the dedication and hard work it takes to become a doctor to ever use one for a cheap thrill.

I was discharged from Jefferson rehab with a rented wheelchair and a black quad-based cane. Using the chair helped my walking ability not a bit, and the cane was awkward to carry around. So, I held my arms out to the side and in front of me, for balance when I walked. I looked like Frankenstein's monster in the old movies as I lurched about. The Frankenstein lurch. That was me. And I made people nervous because it looked as if I were in imminent danger of falling. The ever present halo added to the surrealism of it all.

In his back yard Philip rigged up a walkway for me. He ran two parallel lengths of taut, inch-thick rope about waist high and two and half feet apart. It was about thirty feet long, and I practiced walking between the ropes knowing they were there should I lose my balance. Balance was a problem, and I was always afraid of falling, but the ropes gave me confidence.

Philip was keen on physical fitness, and besides having a Schwinn Airdyne stationary bike, had a weight bench, and a full complement of free weights. I gradually worked myself up to twenty five minutes, three times a week on the bike.

Brother Phil

Two and a half months after my injury and six weeks since entering rehabilitation, I still was not strong enough to bench press the weight bar. Just the bar, no weights. Before I mastered the bar, Philip added a couple small weights. He encouraged me, pushed me, and I wanted to please him, and myself. My head quivered with the effort of trying to push the bar off my chest and extend my arms.

My head was shaking almost imperceptibly within the halo frame when I heard a small popping noise, like the sound of something going through bone. Only much later after the seizures and the head x-rays did I realize what had happened.

Ninety days after the halo and brace had been put on, my brother, Dave, and I went to see Doctor Cotler, the orthopedic surgeon, in hopes of having the halo removed. I sorely wanted to be rid of it. For the preceding month I'd been doing isometric exercises to prepare my neck for the halo to be removed. Doctor Cotler shook my hand and complimented me on my grip strength. He then told me the x rays that he'd taken showed there was some slippage in the stabilization work that had been done. The halo would need to stay on for another thirty days.

Brother Dave

Big, big disappointment. I needed to go home. My brother and his family were nothing but good to me while I stayed with them, but they are very tidy people, and I'm an "Oscar" kind of guy. As long as it doesn't get to be unhealthy, a little mess is okay with me. Even when something did hit the floor, I wasn't fast enough to get there first. Three weeks of me, and now another four. It wasn't fair to them.

I spent the month continuing to get stronger, and this time when I was taken to see Doctor Cotler, he gave the okay for the halo to be removed. We were directed to the cast room for its removal. There was nothing about the technician to suggest he didn't know what he was doing, but he kept trying to remove a nut by turning it in the wrong direction. I could hear and feel the metal being stressed when my brother said, "The nut needs to be turned the other way." The technician tried it, and everything proceeded smoothly from then on. The tech was an older, experienced guy, and I don't how he could have made such an error, except we must have made him nervous.

One morning early on at my brother Philip's house, I had been working out on the weight bench and was trying to get up when I fell to the floor. I thought I lost consciousness as well, so I called the hospital and went in to get checked out. They said I had an episode of syncope, a drop in blood pressure resulting in a temporary loss of consciousness. That sounded reasonable.

On my last night at my brother's house I was lying on the couch in the living room. Phil and his wife, Deb, had just gone to bed. As I lay there I had an overwhelming sense of falling off the couch and put my arm out to break my fall. When I hit the floor my arm slapped it with a noticeable bang. My sister-in-law, who happens to be a registered nurse, investigated, and saw me convulsing on the floor. When I regained consciousness she told me what she had seen, and said she needed to call an ambulance. I felt fine and made light of the entire incident. I didn't need an ambulance or a hospital. Philip said, "What if it were me convulsing on the floor, what would you do?" He had me with that, and there was nothing left to say except, "Call the ambulance."

The ambulance came to my brother's house, and it was decided I would go with them. As we were in Jersey, the ambulance crew wanted to take me to the local hospital, but I was insistent on them taking me over the Ben Franklin bridge to Philly, and then on to the Jefferson emergency room.

I was respectful and afraid of the seriousness of what had happened to me so far, and needed to be where people best understood my condition. For whatever the hell was wrong with me now I needed to be back at Jefferson. It was November 26, and I had been with my brother for seven weeks. It was four and a half months since I crashed.

While being observed in the emergency room I had another seizure. I have no recollection of the seizures, but by reading over my medical records from that time, some memories from my brother's house were jostled. I remember my mouth filling with saliva and my jaw flapping up and down on its own volition. From reading my records I understand each episode lasted one or two minutes during which my body shook all over. My eyes were open, but not reactive.

The emergency room doctors determined I was having focal point seizures. A CT scan of my head revealed a perforation of the skull at the right pin site and a brain abscess. I was scheduled for surgery the next morning. A burr hole, started with a hand drill, was made and the site drained. The infected area was copiously flushed with antibiotics. I mostly felt okay, but in the following days continued to have excess saliva, slurred speech, and my eyes were out of whack.

Lab cultures of infected brain tissue showed light growth of three different bacteria. One was staph, another E. coli. I was immediately started on large doses of two different antibiotics.

One was ceftazidime, two grams every eight hours. The other antibiotic varied and was not effective. The neurosurgeons wanted to use penicillin, but because I had gotten light-headed once as a teenager after receiving a shot of it, they were hesitant. The CT scans showed the abscess was not resolving, so they decided to desensitize me to penicillin.

After a few days in ninth floor neurology my right knee swelled up, and became too painful to bear any weight. I was put on strict bed rest, had the knee tapped for fluid analysis, and was given thigh high compression boots to wear. How I hated them.

It was all a rude awakening. I was happy and motivated, ambulating without any aids and getting ready to go home. Now I was back in the hospital, unable to walk, with a brain infection that wasn't getting any better, and preparing to receive a medication that could send me into shock. Happy days were never here. The little bit of muscle I'd been able to build up through three and a half months of physical rehabilitation melted away as I laid there. It was very discouraging. From the very beginning of this adventure I'd been able to find reserves of strength to deal with the set backs as they came along, but now I had no more.

There were several doctors looking in on me during this period, but the neurosurgeons were by far the fastest. They were in and out of my room before the dust could settle and generally were not very helpful. There was a pretty, young, black doctor from infectious diseases who came by daily, and one day listened to my tale of woe about not having any more fight left. Thereafter, when she came by she would visit a while, and talk with me about herself. I learned, for instance, that she was from the south. It was only when she saw I was getting a bit of a crush on her, she stopped coming around. When I inquired after her with the doctor who replaced her he said, "I will give her your love."

The nurses showed their ingenuity during my days of bed rest by surrounding me with adult sized diapers, and giving me a bath in bed, including washing my hair. The problem with my knee cleared on its own without my ever knowing what it was or what had caused it.

The penicillin desensitization came off without a hitch and penicillin therapy was begun immediately. Because the antibiotic therapy was expected to take six weeks, it was decided to make a more permanent intravenous port than the one on my arm.

A Hickman catheter was placed high up on the right side of my chest allowing direct access to a major vein. The catheter surgery itself felt like someone was leaning on my chest for a couple hours. When my brother, Don, asked me afterward how the surgery went, I told him it was no worse than a good punch in the mouth. He laughed and thought it a good analogy.

At the time I did not understand the cause and effect of the seizure activity, but with the benefit of hindsight, there is understanding now where there was none before. Weeks earlier at my brother's house, I passed out and fell off the weight bench. The doctors thought it was an episode of syncope, a drop in blood pressure.

Actually, that was the first seizure. I was incontinent with urine when that happened, but no one made the connection. The first week that I was with my brother, and my head was quivering with the strain of trying to bench press the weight bar, I heard a small popping noise, like something going through bone. That is when the right, front pin perforated my skull and allowed bacteria to enter. That was the beginning of my abscess.

After the Hickman catheter had been put in place and the antibiotics were being properly infused, the question arose as to what to do with me. Except for the administration of the drugs every six and eight hours, I didn't need to be in the hospital, and the hospital didn't want me there. Once again an effort was made to get me into the program at the McGee Institute, and again my insurance company refused to pay. This time, however, I was glad. McGee worked with recently paralyzed people, patients who had completed rehabilitation, but needed help with wheelchair skills, activities of daily living, and generally maximizing their abilities. My condition had improved so dramatically, I would have felt out of place.

The hospital wanted to send me home to self administer the medications. They had me try to do it, but my fingers had no fine motor skills and couldn't begin to manipulate the things necessary to make it all work.

Their next suggestion was for me to go back to Philip and his family, and have my sister-in-law, whom they remembered was a registered nurse, give me the medications. I had to explain to them that my sister-in-law, Debbie, works for a living, had a family to take care of, and couldn't reasonably be expected to give me two different drugs every six and eight hours. Not to mention the imposition of having me live with them again. It was something the staff hadn't considered. One thing was sure, ninth floor neurology was determined to be rid of me.

In the meanwhile, Jeff, my physical therapist from my first admission, was taking me down to the third floor to do therapy in the gym. The rehabilitation unit was also on the third floor, as was Donna, the charge nurse. As far as nurses went, she was the best. She had the best education, the most experience, and the desire and ability to be an outstanding nurse. And she was.

It was my good fortune that she took a liking to me, but more than that, she believed in me. Somehow, she had gotten word of my predicament with neurology and had me transferred back to rehab, in my old room, even my old bed. Donna knew how to get things done, and I loved her for it. In spite of the special treatment, it was hard still to be in the hospital.

I took as much gym time as possible, and would go out on a day pass on weekends. Often, one of my siblings would take me on an outing, or I would go walking around center city Philadelphia. I had a small tape player, and my daughter had given me a tape of "The Traveling Wilburys". It was great music for walking, and I thoroughly enjoyed both, the music and the walking. I felt a little vulnerable due to my physical condition, but at least the halo was gone, as was the stiff Philadelphia collar that followed it.

The hospital was located a half dozen blocks from the historic part of the city. I was somewhat familiar with the area, because as a high school kid I had a part time job working for a silversmith on Sansom Street. Sansom Street, otherwise known as "jewelers' row", bordered the historic area.

On one of the occasions when Rita came to see me, we walked for ten or fifteen blocks among very old, immaculately kept homes and shops. It was a very classy area. We were on our way to a Philadelphia seafood landmark, "Old Original Bookbinders", to have a bowl of their specialty, clam chowder. The walk turned out to be longer than anticipated, and my injured bladder was telling me it had to be relieved, or I was going to wet myself.

In this very proper, historic area, there was an eighteenth century church with a full cemetery behind it. Against every instinct, and hoping no one would see me, I walked around the low stone wall, entered the graveyard and quietly relieved myself behind a very weather worn tombstone. There was no choice. We quickly put a couple blocks behind us. It was a lesson learned with my injured bladder.

During the day I would sometimes go to the hospital solarium. They had a grill and I could get a good cheese steak hoagy there. I grew up eating cheese steaks and had missed them living in New York.

At night I would often take the elevator up to the thirteenth floor and go to the enclosed patio there. Sometimes there were a few of us, but mostly it was just me. Rarely was anyone else around. I would sit in one of the chairs and look out on the city and the lower roofs of the hospital complex. Honestly, it wasn't much of a view. Three times I saw a medical evacuation helicopter land on one of the lower buildings, and watched the medics scurry out and bring in the injured.

When it was time to go back to my room, I would take the stairs and walk the ten flights to the ward. Walking the stairs was good for me, and it gave me a few more minutes out of my room. The stairwell was right across from the door to my room, and I was able to avoid the bright lights of the nursing station.

One of my last roommates was a young black kid about sixteen years old. He had only recently become paralyzed for life from a gunshot wound. He took his condition like it was just another day. Although newly injured, he was highly skilled with using a wheelchair. He could, for instance, balance the chair on its back wheels. I asked him how he became so good using a wheelchair. He told me he learned from his cousin, who had been shot and paralyzed a few years earlier. He was a very ethnic kid, from "old Philadelphia". I liked him, really felt for him. He used to tease me for "trying to sing." I gave him my book on paralysis when I left.

۞

HOME AGAIN

CT scans were routinely used to see how the brain abscess was doing, and all showed it to be resolving. The expected six weeks of antibiotic therapy lasted seven weeks and two days, and then I was homeward bound.

The very thought scared the hell out of me. I had been in the hospital for five months, and away from home for over six. The home I had to return to was awful. It had been a fixer-upper when I bought it, and I'd only had time to get it cleaned out. That was a big improvement, but the place was still bad. The small story-and-a-half house had been sectioned off into many small areas using ugly, mismatched paneling shoddily applied. The kitchen area was full of flimsy metal cabinets covered in godawful yellow contact paper. It was hard even to think about.

The night before being discharged I left the hospital and went to the bar across the street, where I bought a pack of cigarettes. My nearly seven months of being tobacco free were over, and just like that, I was back on the drag for years to come.

I was discharged to home on January 21, 1989, six and a half months after crashing my vehicle. Being home was hard. I was used to having things done for me, my needs met by others. At home it was just me. The doctors said I was good to go, I needed no further therapy. I knew better. I was weak and walked as if I were drunk. The irony didn't escape me. Also, for the first time since the accident, I was badly bothered with pain. When I called the hospital, they said to do my home care exercises. My needs were so much greater than that.

I made an appointment with Otsego Orthopedics in Oneonta which specialized in sports medicine and had a well equipped exercise room. I explained my history and pain problem to Doctor Elting, the orthopedic surgeon who ran the place, and he agreed with my assessment of the need to get strong. He assigned my care to the physical therapists who worked for him.

At last, I was going to get the exercise I had thought I needed all along. It was the beginning of the hard work I had to do in order to reclaim my physical self. Orthopedics had a dozen or so fitness machines, each working a different part of the body. I worked all but one and added weight or resistance as often as possible. I worked out for a full hour and my pulse was pounding by the time I finished. Several things were tried to help me with pain: ultra sound, massage, whirlpool, cortisone injections, electrical nerve stimulation. Nothing was of any enduring value. Doctor Elting, who supervised my care, said of my time there, "He is a very courageous individual who has done a wonderful job of helping himself." I needed to get strong again. Otsego Orthopedics helped a lot.

After finishing my workout at Orthopedics I would walk the half mile to Fox Hospital. I had earlier introduced myself to Ron Longo, who was in charge of the occupational/physical therapy unit of the hospital. I told him my history, the problems I had, and the things I needed help with. He said he could see the pain in my eyes and was determined to do all he could to help.

Pain is a curious condition, and often the best that can be done for it is to be fit and limber. Ron was a decent sort, and if my forty-five minute session ran to an hour and a half, that was fine with him. One of the stretching exercises he had me do for my shoulder was to turn a large adjustable wheel that was mounted on the wall. Every time it would start to get easy for me, he would adjust the wheel upward. It hurt a bit, but helped maximize the range of motion on my left side. My hands needed a lot of work. They were weak and had almost no fine motor skills. Ron rigged up a weight and pulley system in which I would lift the weight using only one finger. Every digit got a turn. I exercised like that for the months I was with him.

I probably have as much time invested in my fingers and hands as in the rest of my body put together. Ron was pleased with the results. I had more than doubled my grip strength, from twenty to forty four pounds in one hand, and from twenty to fifty two in the other.

Therapy days were Monday, Wednesday, and Friday, and they were seriously exhausting. Even the next day I was too tired to do anything besides feed myself and do my personal care. Sunday was the only day I had energy enough to engage life.

There were some well meaning people who told me the fatigue I experienced was only a plateau, and that it would pass. It never did.

The cord injury changed my life, and fatigue is one of the ways. The closest I've come to understanding it is this: the nerves in our body are sheathed in a substance called myelin, which increases the speed at which impulses are conducted. The myelin in the body parts that were paralyzed and now recovered was degraded, leading to nerve and muscle fatigue. It is most pronounced in the large muscles on the front of my legs. I have lawn chairs scattered about outside for when I take my breaks and need to get off my feet.

Before my injury I could put in a full day's work, and was happy to do so. After the injury I could only work for three or four hours, but was very happy to do so.

One of my roommates during my second stay at rehab was a man in his mid sixties named George. He had fallen from a stepladder while changing a light bulb, injuring his back and spinal cord. He was retired and had been helping someone out when he fell. He spoke often about his deceased wife, and how they had renovated and restored an old mill house and waterwheel to working order . To hear him tell it, she was the brains and drive behind the project; he was only her helper. I never heard anyone speak so respectfully and admiringly of another person as George did of his wife. He had been a hard worker in life and no different when it came to helping himself get better.

Those who put the most into their recovery got the most out of it. It wasn't luck. It was focus and effort. George was so obviously a good man; it practically emanated from him. I knew he was a good guy, but he wasn't so sure about me. Once when Rita was visiting she spent quite a bit of time with George while I was participating in a news event the rehab unit was having. He later told me, "You'd be a damn fool to let her get away." I had a lot of respect for George.

In fact, Rita continued to be a blessing in my life. She had bought a small house in Worcester when I was still at Wilson Hospital in Johnson City. It was a half block from the group home for developmentally disabled adults where she worked. I used to work at the same group home and it's where we met. She didn't drive at the time, but an older gentleman in her neighborhood would transport her to my house for a small fee. She usually came on her days off, and besides cooking for me, would busy herself tidying the house and generally being helpful.

I continued with therapy at Fox Hospital and Otsego Orthopedics until August of '89, thirteen months since it all began. I was, in the main, as good as I was going to get. I was pleased with what had been accomplished. Not only could I walk; it wasn't particularly obvious I had a disability. I've always been grateful for that.

One time when my brother, Philip, his wife, Debbie, and I were getting in the car to go somewhere, and I was still in the wheelchair, Debbie said to Philip, "Can he get in the car by himself?" I was close enough to touch her, but she addressed her question to him, like I wasn't there. I realized then that one of the worst things about being disabled would be the reactions of other people.

After finishing with the therapies, my body worked pretty well. I was independent with my bowel and bladder and sexually whole again. Nothing about me worked as well as it used to, but everything worked, and for that - grateful doesn't cover it.

I was grateful, too, to the country I was a part of. The whole affair was very costly to me. My fairly new, paid for truck was a total loss. Except for food, all my living expenses continued while I was away: child support, taxes, insurance, heat, electric, and phone. The fixed wing air ambulance with registered nurse on board from

Binghamton, NY to Philadelphia, PA was very expensive. In short, I was broke

When I first got to Jefferson the social worker there had a social security representative come to the hospital and take an application from me for disability benefits. Six months later it was approved. If it wasn't for social services hauling me back and forth from home into Oneonta for therapy for more than four months, I could never have done what I did. I owned my house outright, but if it wasn't for the social safety net, I would have lost everything.

So, while I had significant disability, I was far from useless. I always knew I would regain the ability to walk, but never thought I'd be able to climb around on the old barn again. The barn is gone now, I took it down one board at a time, and put a much smaller building, framed with the barn salvage, in its place.

The old barn

The building that replaced the old barn,

The work was good for me. It kept me in shape and kept my mind off my discomfort. I couldn't stay with it for more than three or four hours a day, but I could do it every day, week in, week out. Ever so gradually things got done, even big projects. My home became a more comfortable and pleasant place to be.

Recovering from paralysis gave me great confidence in what I could do physically, and I wanted to celebrate that somehow. During the four weeks in intensive care I pretty much looked over my life. I realized that my most pleasant memories were of the times spent on the water in a canoe. I decided to try to paddle on the Susquehanna River from my area in upstate New York down to the Chesapeake Bay in Maryland.

Rita became my house mate, and with her help I bought a two-person folding kayak. When the boat was disassembled it fit into two bags. I chose a kayak because my left shoulder is badly injured and I wanted to stress my upper body evenly. I practiced paddling on the upper Susquehanna and Unadilla rivers. I planned carefully and tried to think of every contingency.

I put in at the confluence of the Unadilla and Susquehanna rivers. I had paddled most of the water up river but none of it down river. It rained so hard before leaving that my departure was delayed a day. The river was bank high and the current strong.

I paddled from morning until early afternoon, when I would start looking for a camp site. Finding a good site was always a priority. I generally camped on islands, or along the banks, although my fourth night was in a Holiday Inn. What a luxury that shower was!

Sixteen days after putting in, I arrived at the Conowingo Dam in the state of Maryland. The down river side of the dam was tidewater and the beginning of the bay. There my paddle ended. The people at the dam were obliged to provide portage around the dam. A couple of young men came in a pickup truck and hauled me and my boat to a nearby state park. It rained that night, the first hard rain of the trip. The next morning I called a cab, and with my boat in its two bags and my backpack of other belongings, I went to the bus station in Baltimore, to begin the long ride home.

The sixteen days on the river constitute the best adventure of my life. I doubt I would ever have attempted such a thing had I not experienced the cord injury and the attendant recovery from it.

In the ensuing years I've lived a somewhat physical life, trying to stay healthy and fit. It's probably been the best way to treat my condition, and the lifestyle has suited me well. Before Vietnam, psychedelic drug use, and that time in our country's social history, what I wanted for my life was an education in psychology and whatever that might bring. Afterward, however, what I wanted was a house in the country, a piece of land to take care of, and the time to do it. My injury gave me the time. So, in a back ass-ward way, and not without a few caveats, I had achieved the life I wanted.

I've not distinguished myself in any way, but I've enjoyed using my body and not wasting what I so nearly lost. I spent the twentieth anniversary of my injury at a remote Adirondack lake lean-to that took three days of paddling and portaging to get to. In the summer of my sixty-fifth year I spent a week on my bicycle, pedaling two hundred seventy miles around central New York and along the Erie canal.

Adirondack Park
Northern Forest Canoe Trail

There is an appreciation for life that wasn't there before, and I feel so very lucky for all I have been able to experience. Not least of all, except for the occasional social drink, I have put alcohol behind me. For too many years I was an accident waiting to happen. Now it is done.

Vertebrae

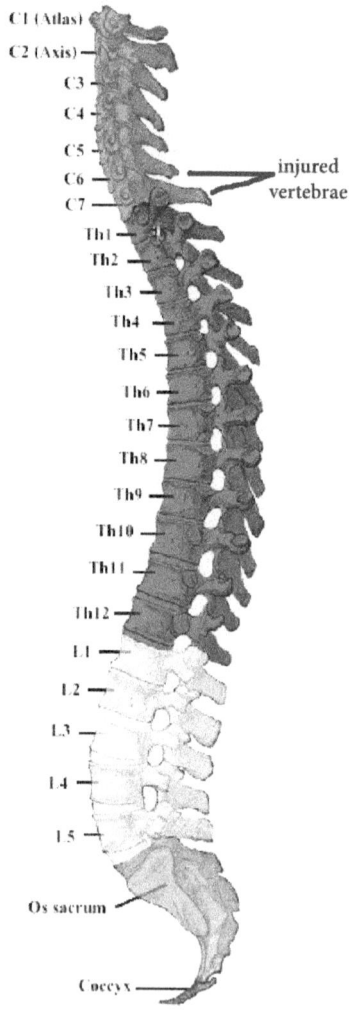

Cervical (neck) injuries (C1 to C8)

C1 - Atlas - The Atlas is the topmost vertebra, and along with C2, forms the joint connecting the skull and spine. Its chief peculiarity is that it has no body, and this is due to the fact that the body of the atlas has fused with that of the next vertebra.

C2 - Axis - Forms the pivot upon which C1 rotates. The most distinctive characteristic of this bone is the strong odontoid process (dens) which rises perpendicularly from the upper surface of the body. The body is deeper in front than behind, and prolonged downward anteriorly so as to overlap the upper and front part of the third vertebra. Injuries to C-1 and C-2 can result in a loss of many involuntary functions, including the ability to breathe, necessitating breathing aids such as ventilators or diaphragmatic pacemakers.

C-3 - Injury to spinal bone three often causes pain, tingling, and sometimes numbness in the arms, neck, and head. If the fourth cervical vertebrae (C4) nerve root is also involved, pain is usually felt in the upper arms and shoulders, as well as the lower neck.

<u>C4</u> - Cervical Vertebra - Quadriplegia and breathing difficulty - The fourth cervical (neck) vertebra from the top. Injuries above the C-4 level may require a ventilator for the person to breathe properly.

<u>C5</u> - Quadriplegia with some shoulder and elbow function - 5th cervical vertebrae down from the base of the skull, found in the neck. C5 injuries often maintain shoulder and biceps control, but have no control at the wrist or hand.

C5 to C8 injuries - Corresponding nerves control the arms and hands, a person with this level of spinal injury may still be able to breathe on their own and speak normally.

<u>C6 -</u> Cervical Vertebra - Quadriplegia with shoulder, elbow, and some wrist function - The sixth cervical (neck) vertebra from the top. The next-to-last of the seven cervical vertebrae. An injury to the spinal cord between C6 and C7 vertebrae is called a C6-7 injury. These injuries generally allow wrist control, but no hand function.

__C7__- **Vertebra Prominens - Quadriplegia with shoulder, elbow, wrist, and some hand function** - The most distinctive characteristic of this vertebra is the existence of a long and prominent spinous process, hence the name vertebra prominens. In some subjects, the seventh cervical vertebra is associated with an abnormal pair of ribs, known as cervical ribs. These ribs are usually small, but may occasionally compress blood vessels (such as the subciavian artery) or nerves in the brachial plexus, causing unpleasant symptoms. C-7 and T-1 can straighten their arms but still may have dexterity problems with the hand and fingers. Injuries at the thoracic level and below result in paraplegia, with the hands not affected.

__C8__ - Quadriplegia with normal arm function; hand weakness - Although there are seven cervical vertebrae (C1-C7), there are eight cervical nerves (C1-C8). All nerves except C8 emerge above their corresponding vertebrae, while the C8 nerve emerges below the C7 vertebra. In other words C8 is a nerve root not a vertebrae.

☙❧

SARA - INSIGHT

She was dull black all over with a shaggy head and a full bushy tail. When she wagged her tail, which she often did, the wag would start at the tip of her tail and work its way to her shoulders until her whole body was shaking. She looked a buffoon and, for such a large dog, not the least intimidating.

My farmer neighbor said to me one day in reference to the dog, "I wanted to see what the fool was up to." As it turned out, the fool was up to chasing down and killing woodchucks.

Woodchucks dig large burrows and tunnels when they excavate for their homes. The heavy equipment the farmers use in the fields can break through these excavations and become damaged. So, Sara's routing out and killing these animals was good for the farm. Thereafter, the neighbor instructed area hunters to not shoot my dog even if she was running deer. Sara didn't chase deer, but it was comforting to know that even if she did, she would come home to me.

Some years after the dog died the neighbor's wife told me Sara used to come to their back door every morning looking for a treat, and they obliged her.

When she was a year old she killed one of the chickens that we kept for eggs. It had been scratching around the back yard one morning when she grabbed hold of it and ended its life. I had a shovel in my hands when it happened and hit her with the back side of it high up on her back leg. I hit her hard enough to knock her side ways, but she never killed another chicken after that. However, if a chicken got on the back porch she would make it fly off. That afternoon she brought home her first woodchuck.

One day while drinking beer at the top of the field, I watched her catch a woodchuck. Instead of running for the chuck, she ran for the hole. When she got there first, it was game over.

About the Author

The author spent his boyhood and young adulthood in a small southern New Jersey town along the Delaware river. He served his country as a medic in the Army from 1968 through 1970, including a tour of duty in Vietnam.

He moved to south central New York in 1973 where he finished course work for his bachelor's degree. He has been a resident of Otsego County, NY, for more than forty years and has lived on Bell Hill since 1987.

He is an avid gardener and grows produce the year round in his attached greenhouse. He enjoys the quiet and solitude of paddling on the local creeks, and occasionally likes to turn a phrase and have fun with words.

The Author in VietNam

Barn Salvage

 *One of my gardens.*

*The author and Rita on the occasion of their marriage.
Isn't Rita beautiful?*

*Me and my siblings in birth order, left to right:
Philip, Me, Don, Dave and Nancy
July, 2000*

ACKNOWLEDGEMENTS

Front Cover Illustration:
From Shutterstock.com

Stryker, Halo and brace illustrations were
obtained from internet research.*

Photographs:
All but Mr. Dunn's portrait photo were
taken by Bruce Dunn, used with permission.

Bruce Dunn's portrait:
by Frank Treacy
of Costa Studios, in Oneonta, NY.

* If it it discovered that we owe a royalty for any illustration usage,
we apologize and will consider compensation.

Thank you for reading.

Do share this with anyone who might benefit.

To Order This Book

From Amazon:
Title: My Path Through Paralysis
Author: Bruce Dunn

From the Author:
email: bpdunn@frontiernet.net
188 Bell Hill Road, Morris, NY 13808.

To Schedule a Visit

The author is available to talk, encourage, and discuss, mornings and afternoons, no evenings. Email us with requests.

NOTE: Book bulk orders may be discounted, email your request.

www.ingramcontent.com/pod-product-compliance
Lightning Source LLC
Chambersburg PA
CBHW071721040426
42446CB00011B/2163